The first pillar of faith in Islam is Belief in Allah. As Muslims, we believe in Allah in accordance with His beautiful names and attributes. Allah has revealed His names repeatedly in the Holy Quran primarily for us to understand who He is.

Learning and memorizing the names of Allah will help us to identify the correct way to believe in Him. There is nothing more sacred and blessed than understanding the names of Allah and living by them. How do we expect to worship, love and trust our Lord, The Almighty Allah, if we don't know who He is?

Allah says in the Quran:

"And to Allah belong the best names, so invoke Him by them.. (Quran 7:180)
"He is Allah, the Creator, the Inventor, the Fashioner; to Him belong the best names. (Quran 59:24)

Below we put together a coloring book to learning the meaning and benefits of the 99 names of Allah.

In this book, we have combined the symmetrical beauty of mandalas with the 99 names of Allah written in Arabic calligraphy.

Enjoy your learning , enjoy your coloring moment , God bless you all dear brothers and sisters.

Allah / الله / Allah

ٱلْمُتَكَبِّرُ | AL-MUTAKABBIR | The Supreme, The Majestic -

ٱلْجَبَّارُ | AL-JABBAR | The Compeller, The Restorer -

ٱلْمُصَوِّرُ - | AL-MUSAWWIR | The Fashioner
- ٱلْغَفَّارُ | AL-GHAFFAR | The All- and Oft-Forgiving

ٱلْمُصَوِّرُ | AL-MUSAWWIR | The Fashioner
- ٱلْغَفَّارُ | AL-GHAFFAR | The All- and Oft-Forgiving

ٱلْقَهَّار

ٱلْوَهَّاب

ٱلْمُذِلُّ | AL-MUZIL | The Dishonourer, The Humiliator -
ٱلْسَّمِيعُ | AS-SAMEE' | The All-Hearing -

الْمُقِيتُ

الْحَسِيبُ

ٱلْوَاسِعُ | AL-WAASI' | The All-Encompassing, the Boundless

ٱلْحَكِيمُ | AL-HAKEEM | The All-Wise

اَلْوَدُودُ | AL-WADOOD | The Most Loving –
اَلْمَجِيدُ | AL-MAJEED | The Glorious, The Most Honorable –

اَلْوَدُودُ | AL-WADOOD | The Most Loving –
اَلْمَجِيدُ | AL-MAJEED | The Glorious, The Most Honorable –

ٱلْحَقُّ | AL-HAQQ | The Absolute Truth -
ٱلْوَكِيلُ | AL-WAKEEL | The Trustee, The
Disposer of Affairs -

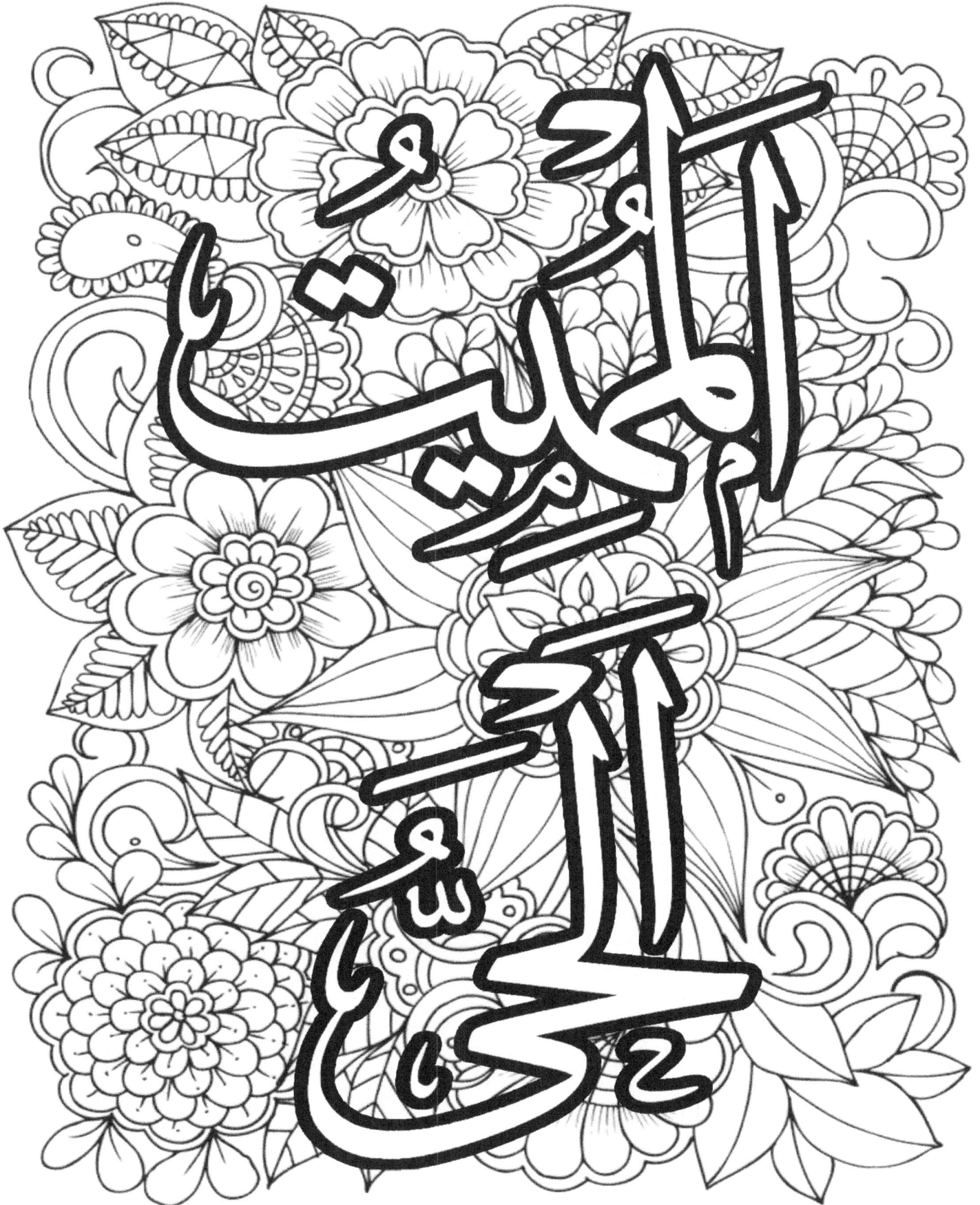

ٱلْتَّوَّابُ

ٱلْمُنْتَقِمُ

مَالِكُ ٱلْمُلْكُ | MAALIK-UL-MULK | Master of the Kingdom, Owner of the Dominion –

– ذُو ٱلْجَلَالِ وَٱلْإِكْرَامُ | DHUL-JALAALI WAL-IKRAAM | Possessor of Glory and Honour, Lord of Majesty and Generosity

الرشيد

الصبور

Made in United States
North Haven, CT
25 June 2025